Friendly Street
NEW POETS 16

§

Friendly Street
NEW POETS 16

Voyages to Another Planet • John Brydon

Mistaken for a Real Poet • Mike Hopkins

Glowing in the Dark • Simon J. Hanson

§

Friendly Street Poets

Friendly Street Poets Inc.
PO Box 3697
Norwood SA 5067
friendlystreetpoets.org.au

Wakefield Press
1 The Parade West
Kent Town
South Australia 5067
www.wakefieldpress.com.au

First published 2011

Cover photograph copyright © Thom Sullivan
Cover design by Clinton Ellicott, Wakefield Press, and
Thom Sullivan, Friendly Street Poets Inc.
Typeset by Clinton Ellicott, Wakefield Press
Edited by Thom Sullivan, Friendly Street Poets Inc.
Printed in Australia by Griffin Digital, Adelaide

ISBN 978 1 86254 965 4

Friendly Street Poets Inc. is supported
by the South Australian Government
through Arts SA.

Contents

Edited by
Thom Sullivan

Voyages to Another Planet

John Brydon

John Brydon is a scientist, photographer and consulting engineer, working in industry and with the local universities. He was born in London, migrated to Australia in 1988 and has lived in Adelaide for about six years. His interests include anything and everything.

Acknowledgements

Some of these poems, or earlier versions of them, have appeared in *Friendly Street Poets: Thirty* and *Friendly Street Poets 31: Unruly Sun* and *ArtState* No. 10. The third section of *Discovery Trilogy* was highly commended in the *2010 Great Big Science Read Sci-ku* competition sponsored by Friendly Street Poets and RiAus.

Dedication
To April, for whom nine lives were not enough.

Contents

The Embalming of Ultima Pavior

A children's park in the Western suburbs,
down past the lights and across from the shops,
behind the fence on a grassy corner,
finishing touches to a new attraction.

Ultima Pavior,
master of the road gangs,
king of the tarmac lads,
sits, paralysed, drive-decoupled, engine-less,
degreased and sandblasted,
naked more than ever he has known,
slowly choking as the thick, bright, new paint
settles hard into his joints.

"I have seen pass the generations of roadies,
rough men with big hands,
ageing quickly in the tar smoke,
slow to think and quick to fight.
The mutes and the loud men,
ready with a curse
or a joke behind the foreman's back.

"Daily we fought
with fire and muscle and iron,
the tar, resisting first, but yielding,
always yielding in the end –
all roads once felt the justice of my tread.

"Friday came when the boys went off to their beer,
but next week Paddy had a new job.
And two years then, rusting in the puddled yard,
tractor pushed, but always further from the gate.
Hope calcining every steamless day.

"Never again to feel the cool flow of oil
past bearings hardened bright with daily work.
And, in cold mornings, hot sparks
as my fires bit deep into the damp coke.

"Better I had followed the others to the scrap,
to the quick, searing torch and oblivion.
Better than this pharonic limbo,
stripped and draped in gaudery,
mute witness to another age,
with an itch I cannot scratch
and eyes I cannot close."

The Seventh Wave

No, she said, I shall not swim again.
You do not know how close
I was to drowning, that last time.
I had never seen a wave so big,
it rolled in – always the seventh they say,
it rolled in and slowly, deliberately,
started to take me under.
My legs stopped first, then my arms,
my mouth lower and lower in the water,
I began to slip away, and,
you know what was frightening,
it didn't seem so bad –
to relax and sleep once more.

Then my feet touched the sand,
dragged on a rock,
and the effort was almost too much,
but I made it.
And I lay on the wet sand, gasping,
not quite able to believe it,
but I had endured,
I had become a survivor.

And so, I shall not swim again.
Not they, not you, no-one can guarantee
that the next seventh wave
or the seventieth
or the seven hundredth
will not be the last for me.
So I shall sit here on the beach
(I still like the beach
and from here the sea looks good),
but I shall not swim again,
the waves have ruined it.

And Those Who Laboured

Dusk,
a Chinese city in the South.
The day's work ended
and those who laboured
must now eat.

A restaurant
on the street,
still empty,
the sun not yet down.

A cage
hangs by the door,
a civet
in the cage,
quivering nose,
delicate, fingered paws
gripping the bars.

A pet? In China, no.
This is a country
with customs different
in many ways,
not least, the culinary.

The evening passes.
In the hotel bar,
a resolution:
dollars
for the civet's life,
the crazy *kwailo*
will set his food free.

Out from the hotel,
hurrying
through the wet streets.

The restaurant,
closed,
a cage,
hangs by the door,
empty
as the plates
stacked ready
for the next day's meal.

So Will They Find Me

So, will they find me one day in the gutter,
broken backed, because a driver was late for work
or the kids were playing up in the back seat
or I paused too long for a last scratch.

Will they afford me the courtesy
of a hole in the ground,
a teacloth shroud
and a nice rosebush on top.

Will they shed tears over me
and reminisce the crazy things I did,
laughing that I didn't get caught,
well, not often.

If they will, then,
perhaps it's not such a bad way to go,
just a bit sudden,
with no chance to say goodbye.

A Summer Morning

So, down the stairs I come,
into the morning gloom
to wake the house up.
Drawing the blinds
to let in chattering sunbeams
that never learn to queue.

Opening the door for Gromyko,
who strolls in, replete,
after a night of love and murder.
Chatting to a feathered spokesman
already at the window to discuss terms.

And who's got the cornflakes
'cos I wanted toast.
Is that the time?
Hey, where's my netball top?
I don't know, ask the dog.

Outside, it's warming up
and next door's honeysuckle
chucks its scent over the wall
with neighbourly abandon.

Then, with the rush of puppies,
we all tumble out,
scattering to our daily tasks
and in the sudden quiet of day
Gromyko settles down
to dream about his night.

On His Small Shoulders

Well I'm pregnant, she said,
turning towards the window,
it's confirmed.
I have talked to him for so long in my dreams,
now, soon, I shall see him.

And do you want it?
There is the problem of the ring.
I shall buy one, she said,
for him, I shall buy one.

And your surname?
I shall change it
for him, I shall change it.
He will be ours.

And your family?
They will soften.
With time, they will soften.
He is a baby, they will love him.

And he will remember,
he will remember our happiest times,
of dangers shared and overcome,
of daily life and nightly death.

He will remember the thrill of waking alive
after each raid,
after the explosions and the splintered glass
and the wail of the all-clear.

He will remember the bombs and the sirens,
the smell of plaster and of fresh earth.
I have talked to him for so long
he will remember.

He will carry my hopes,
he will carry my fears,
into a new age.
On his small shoulders will he weigh the past
and with his tiny hands reach forward
for the future.

Out of Africa

Down, then, we came,
thin, new men, walking upright
out of the mountain mists
and into the plains.

Already amongst us,
our Eve,
chosen by some future dice
as our mother through time.

With our clever tongues
and fiery magic,
no simple ape
or gibbering monkey.

And did you see those mammoths
run and fall?
And those big guys,
God, they were dumb.
They never even saw the traps.

With our funny thumbs
and our fiery magic:
Get in our way
and you'll *be the fossil.*

And did you see those Russians
run and fall?
And the others
with the rifles,
they never even saw the tanks.

With our nimble fingers
and social tool making.
Gregarious, ingenious,
each little smith of death.

Bloody Spring

And suddenly
Spring
peeks round the corner
and, Jeez,
it seems like only yesterday
that we were on the slopes at Buller,
Marj and the kids,
without the dog, thank God,
and surely the bloody grass doesn't need cutting again?
And the cat's dumping its winter coat
all over the lounge room suite,
and the wattle birds are banging the grevillea
(who'd be a flower in Spring?)
and the dog's pregnant again
and sometimes this fructification business
is just too much

and I want the summer

and the beach

and a decent bit of ultraviolet

and all the puppies sold off

and a cold beer on the verandah

to build me up again for Autumn.

Sly Thomas

You can understand his surprise,
sly Thomas, creeping up on that bird on the lawn,
edging closer towards a deadly pounce.

You can understand his surprise,
not being able to read well,
relying more on muscular, furry charm than education.

You can understand his surprise,
not having seen the lamppost adverts,
Taekwondo For Pigeons – Liberate Your Inner Eagle.

You can understand his surprise,
the normally fatal lunge countered by a half wing block
feather roll with eye peck riposte.

Now Thomas With The Black Patch
waits grimly for the start of next term.
An early enrolment for *Revenge 101.*

Fortune's Cookie

Fate, being a little bored,
(always a dangerous sign),
pulled the chess game towards her
and picked up another piece.

Couldn't I, just once,
get to make my own moves?
I said.

Why, of course not,
she chuckled,
where would the fun be in that?

Now let's just see what this one does . . .

The Cat Who Sees Ghosts

So, do you see them?
Staring intently as they brush by,
raising a paw in occasional recognition,
chasing them up the hallway,
miaowing at your favourites.

Are there many?
Did they live here?
Were they happy?
We would like answers.

And the cat who sees ghosts
knows,
but doesn't tell.

Sunday, Monday, Museday

Not every day is Museday,
no regular, thirty second of the month,
or the third weekend after Tiffany,
whenever there's a green sunset,
or the flowers bloom out of reason,
or the beer flows uphill
on the sunny side of the street.

No switch it on and turn it up
with digital enhancement and odour free label.
Just a little bell – the insistent chirp of a sparrow
makes me pause for a moment
while a poem, tired of waiting its turn,
jumps out and writes itself down.

(If only I knew who was holding the pen.)

Steps over Familiar Ice

On the coldest day of the year we went skating. The ice was coated with a layer of snow which formed flurries in our wake as we crossed, circled and re-crossed the pond.

Gradually the patterns of our skates on the ice became more intricate so that soon the individual tracks could no longer be discerned.

At dusk we started back. In the twilight we could see that someone had lit a fire in the snow or perhaps it was a reflection.

When the path reached the stile it divided and I walked on alone, listening to the ice beneath my feet, and looking up at the stars.

The Man Who Backed over Death

As soon as I felt the bump I knew: I'd just backed over Death.

After months of complaining, they'd finally put up a mirror in the blind spot but Death, being spectral, just didn't show.

It was Him, of course: the bent sickle poking out from under the car and the skeletal hand.

No sign of his horse though. Only a small steaming pile of equine fright in the roadway.

The bony fingers still grasped a slip of paper – right name, but wrong address. 53B is the *next* driveway, as all the local pizza boys know.

Which maybe explains why a ton and a half of Mercedes travelling backwards at speed round a blind corner came as a bit of a surprise to him.

So, although you can't cheat Death, you can sometimes improve the odds.

And the score was now in my favour, but with Death – I guess – preparing for Round Two.

An Office Sunset

The last fluoro flickers off
to join the others on their perches,
and shadows, held at bay,
now creep out from their lairs.

Talkative terminals stare blankly,
dreaming of future discussions.
Gagged telephones sit hunched and
disconsolate in their corners.

Paperclips cling rustily,
wary of the fate befalling the less tenacious.
Wastepaper baskets placidly chew the cud
as the dust settles on the corpses of rubber bands
that once knew better homes.

Chairs, slumped back, resting from their daylight duties
and cardboard files, paunchy and round shouldered,
look on as,
marshalled by tall cabinets,
who never take time off,
row on row of desks queue patiently for the sunrise.

Nature's Law

After the old cat left on its final visit to the vet all the birds in the garden held a party.

Mind you, it is a bit quiet now, said the blackbird after his third glass of champagne.

And nobody looked at the sparrows in the corner, still mourning a massacred brood.

Yes, it's the survival of the fittest – Nature's Law, said the starling, *only the strongest and clever will survive.*

But because of the drink he was a bit slow to notice the arrival of the new cat.

Which let Nature, who had been fairly quiet up till then, give her views on the subject.

Seasonal Haiku

Buds of Spring burst out
scents of blossoms fill the air
nestlings start to hatch.

Starry Summer sky
evening light's long lasting glow
waving fields of corn.

Autumn days grow short
leaves fall brown from windy trees
gutters fill with rain.

Winter fog descends
snow white frost on window panes
all asleep till Spring.

Apple Pie

Isaac,
you *must* speak to the gardener;
so many of the apples he collected were bruised,
and I just can't make a decent pie with bruised apples.

I mentioned it to him,
but all he kept muttering
was something about
an invisible, mutually attractive force
between the apples and the ground
which accelerated each towards the other.

Dearest,
if you wish apple pie for dinner,
pray speak to the gardener.

Three Birds

Looking into the sunset sky
I could just see three birds,
flying close together,
making their slow progress,
left to right across my view.

As I watched
they seemed to hang there forever,
constant in the deepening glow,
luminous in their permanency.

But I looked away
for a moment,
and my eye returned
to find them . . . to not find them.

Now an empty sky
where angels once played,
darkening
towards a cool, new dawn.

In Another Universe

In another universe,
one of those parallel places that science fiction writers like:

in another universe,
we would not part at the end of the evening and go our
    separate ways.
We would not utter polite thanks for each others' company
that had our hearts racing just by being so close,
and then drift away, back to unbreakable commitments.

In another universe,
we would kiss easily, with the brush of practised lips
and stroll back home, hand in hand,
to our life together,

in another universe.

Discovery Trilogy

Water laps over the bath top,
an ancient Greek
thoughtfully reaches for the soap.

A Summer's day in the orchard,
a mathematician
sits down for a rest.

Photons graze the sun,
the star has moved,
in Princeton, an old man smiles.

Voyage to Another Planet

1. First Contact
Falling through thin air,
the blue sky with a second sun,
the last clouds part to show the land.
Similar,
but more green.

The landing shock then quiet,
senses test the air,
traces of blossoms, half remembered,
or unknown.

One step, then
walking towards the trees.
Sunshine,
laughter by the stream.
Turning to meet me, your arms extending,
smiling, unsure.

Trusting eyes connecting.
Everywhere a bright burning glow,

and now
the Ship
seems
so very far away.

2. The Exchange of Gifts

Along ritual paths
to the place of exchange,
the meeting point of
an unspoken contract,
a small spring
on a magic ley.

Towards the circle
with measured steps of hope,
we carry
bread for life,
steel for strength,
a green branch for renewal.

At the centre,
a pause.
Offer and acceptance.
Bread for life,
steel for strength,
a green branch for renewal.

A step,
a hand
touches an arm,
the sound of running water from the spring,
and in the night air of the valley
a small bird starts to sing.

3. Compline

Grass now covers
the softening hill,
the Mound of the Ship,
no longer clear.

Children's voices,
playing,
a game with rules,
complex
and changing.

The evening air
still warm,

we sit
in the quiet
of heartbeats
long attuned.

Suffer me now this single hour

for the past yet to come

or the future which has been.

Mistaken for a Real Poet

Mike Hopkins

Mike Hopkins was born in Hammersmith, U.K. Not being an adventurous teenager, he unfortunately remembers every second of the 1960s, more for the windswept terraces of football grounds than the sex and psychedelia of swinging London.

He obtained an honours degree in Economics at a second-rate institution, before becoming a computer programmer. The information technology boom allowed him to find work in Wales, Ireland, Zimbabwe, Malawi and ultimately Australia.

He has written a host of dry, boring, occasionally lyrical reports for the South Australian Government, prize winning speeches, left-wing rabble-rousing songs which brought down the Howard Government and, recently, poetry.

Acknowledgements

Some of these poems, or earlier versions of them, have appeared in the Effective Living Centre's anthology *Season of a New Heart*. *Incident at Brownhill Creek* was awarded second prize in the Salisbury Writers' Week Poetry competition (Adult category) and *Caution: This Office May Damage Your Health* was published on the Friendly Street Poets website as 'Best Poem' at the Goolwa reading in April 2010.

Thank You
To Russell Talbot, a fine poet who encouraged me to write poetry in the first place.

To the Poetica group led by Krishan Persaud, for my monthly injection of enthusiasm.

To the Poets' Corner group at ELC, for first mistaking me for a real poet.

Dedication
To my mother, Bridget.

Contents

Memory Loss

drawn upriver from the town
tracing the memory
of a weekend in a cottage
by a creek
waterfowl croaking in the reeds
a rug stretched on the grass
watching
our son's first steps

recognition
flickers
fades

over cottage and grass
the graffiti of a new estate
no birds chatter or trill
bins spill
bottles and food wrappers
a poster:
   free rustic placemat with every 'happy meal'

the small boy lost
in a maze of bricks and bitumen.

Being Mike Ladd

Are you Mike?, said the lady organiser of the poetry gathering,
as I walked through the door
yes, I replied, slightly puzzled as to how she knew my name
oh I AM an admirer of your poetry, she gushed
I struggled to place her, sure I had not met her before
my work must have been circulating spontaneously
maybe it's something to do with the internet
half finished poems on my C drive
slithering their way to the modem
and working their way around Adelaide,
seeking out like minded poetic souls
and saying *Here I am, the work of an underrated,*
    undiscovered talent
being read without my knowledge at open readings
performed at poetry slams by voluptuous women
who sigh at the beauty of my words
and dream of meeting the author
or maybe an acquaintance covertly compiled
a slim compendium of my works
and submitted it to *Faber & Faber*
who eagerly accepted it and printed a first run of
    10,000 copies
of which only a few remain on the shelves of
    Angus & Robertson
having sold out at *Borders*
I wonder when I will receive my royalty cheque
and my invitation to Writers' Week?
my reverie was broken by a stir in the doorway behind me
a man of similar build, a tad younger, a tad more hair,
a far more poetic bearing, walked in
a bevy of admirers surrounded him
the lady organiser looked at me accusingly
marked me down as an impostor
never again will I be mistaken for a real poet.

That Poem about My Mother

Last year, my mother told me the story of her youth
I made it into a poem
containing all of the sorrow and tragedy of her early life
when I think about that poem
I am overwhelmed by sadness
if I try to read it to anyone, I can't make it to the end
yet when I think about my mother
I'm not sad
I visit her from time to time, look at her photograph
talk to her on the phone, email her
without so much as a tear in my eye or a crack in my voice
apart from when I say goodbye.

But the poem about my mother devastates me.

Have I found a way of quarantining pain in a poem?
I'll try writing one about myself
I'll lock it in a safe
alongside the one about my mother
and I'll throw away the key.

Shadow

My shadow has been behaving strangely in recent weeks
I've noticed that it's far less docile than it used to be
for instance, on those occasions when I glimpse
my reflection in a shop window
and see an older, more stooped person than I expect
my shadow is strutting upright, youthful, vigorous
when I'm struggling to run for the bus, heart pounding
my shadow is hurrying ahead, no longer willing to wait for me
I swear last week when cycling, it tried to overtake me
if I'm walking through a crowd, careful not to gaze too long
or longingly at the young women
my shadow is damn well staring and ogling
half turning to follow them
I'm concerned about my shadow's state of mind
I fear it's about to abandon me for a younger model.

Caution: This Office May Damage Your Health

It's the tea room gossip that irks ya
it stings and blinds ya
with its *he said* and *she said*
and *you'll never guess*
and the bloody *oh my God! oh my God!*
what was she thinking?
you thought at first they were all drab and grey
but it turns out the place is like a Bangkok brothel
it's the tea room gossip that irks ya

It's the mobile phone ring tones that needles ya
they frazzles and dulls your brain
bleating from unattended desks
tinny tones of the latest TV soap theme
or over and over some comedy show catch phrase
mildly amusing the first time
irritating the second and then increasingly exasperating
until you swear you'll bring a sledgehammer in tomorrow
and smash the bloody thing to smithereens
it's the mobile phone ring tones that needles ya

It's the meetings that drives ya to distraction
they numbs and deadens ya
the 'purely for decorative purposes' agenda
the action items never to be actioned
the head spinning pointless PowerPoints
with ballistic bullets and apoplectic arrows
meaningless as a mission statement
and sleep inducing presenters talking to the wall
it's the meetings that drives ya to distraction

But it's the clichés that finally does ya head in
they blisters and rips ya
as you're listening to a heads up about world's best practice
getting incentivized to leap from behind the 8 ball
through a 24 by 7 window of opportunity
into a whole new ball game on a level playing field
moving forward, at the end of the day,
in this rapidly changing globalised environment
yes, it's the clichés that finally does ya head in.

Illegal

— On visiting Woomera Detention Centre on Mothers' Day

I am the man you locked up in the desert
this is my wife whom you kept from my side
this is my son who went mad in the desert
this is my daughter whose scars we must hide

this is the cage where we lived in the desert
these are the guards who made sure we complied
this is the hut where we slept in the desert
these are the bars we stared through each night

this was the plan to send us to the desert
this was the way to keep others away
use us like corpses that swing in the desert
making it clear that we are to blame

now we are free from that jail in the desert
now we are told we have paid for our sins
but our souls have been seared by our time in the desert
our minds have been scorched by the sun and the wind.

The Australian Thirteens

– After Maya Angelou's 'The Thirteens'

The Australian Thirteens (Black)

Your mummy took a beating
Your daddy's drinking beer
Your brother's lost his eyesight
Your sister's disappeared
The thirteens. Right On.

Your cousin's sniffing petrol
Your uncle's in the cell
Your buddy's begging money
To spend in the hotel
The thirteens. Right On.

And you, you make me shameful
To see the state you're in
I tell you *live like we do*
But all you do is grin
At
The thirteens. Right On.

The Australian Thirteens (White)

Your mother's hooked on Botox
Your daddy's with the guys
Your sister's anorexic
She fades before your eyes
The thirteens. Right On.

Your daughter is a junkie
Your son beats queers for fun
Your priests molest your children
And you just move them on
The thirteens. Right On.

You living in that city
And buying all that stuff
And still you look unhappy
'Cos you'll never have enough
No
The thirteens. Right On.

Poems 'R' Us

Poems 'R' Us is proud to announce the opening of its Adelaide super store. We have everything the DIY poet needs. Whether you love limericks or have a passion for pantoums, you'll find what you fancy at *Poems 'R' Us*.

We have storage solutions to keep your poems fresh. Home security cameras to protect you from plagiarists. Trimmers and pruners for cutting those odes down to size. Fencing products to stop your free verse running amok. Signs for your gate – *Beware of the Doggerel*. Trendy ear muffs for sensitive family members when you're practicing those performance pieces. Trouble with your enjambment? – our line trimmers are just the thing. Going out the door like hot haiku is our cone of silence, designed to fit perfectly over your teenage rap artist.

If building poems from scratch is not your thing we have an extensive range of flat pack poems that fit easily into the boot of your car – you can take them home and put them together using just a few simple literary devices. You can even purchase lengths of poetry by the metre or the foot.

Deposit your surplus stanza, leftover line or redundant rhyme in our recycling bin. Your cast offs are reassembled good as new. Then we distribute them to disadvantaged people living below the poetry line. At our trade-in counter you can swap your old poems for shiny new ones. And we promise to make a fair and reasonable offer for all poems in good working order.

So remember:

> *Epic or epigram*
> *Sestina or sonnet*
> *Poems 'R' Us*
> *Has the tools to work on it.*

Zambezi

We cowered by the fire together
banging billies, cursing the dark
the dark where, now and then,
on either side of us
hot coal eyes would burn, blink and disappear
followed by a mounting roar
a foul smell of urine carried on the night breeze
intended to make us panic and run
into the maw of the she-lion downwind
we fed the fire and huddled closer
cursed louder, banged harder
until, minute by minute, hour by hour
dawn approached
and the lions tired of their game
leaving their sleepless playthings
to our smouldering, cursing hysteria.

I'm in Love with the Television News Reader

7 pm every evening she appears
in my living room, bringing me the news of the world
Juanita Cox looking at me with her large eyes,
gently tossing her coiffured blond hair
demurely enunciating ugly words
through her beautifully shaped mouth

another insane event has occurred in some far off country
and Juanita Cox has red lip gloss on tonight
another boat load of desperate people has reached our shores
only Juanita can make the word *asylum* sound erotic
another paedophile released on bail
you shouldn't have to read such filth Juanita
more bikie gang trouble in the city
if I had tats and a Harley, Juanita, would you ride off
    with me?
the Government's economic policies are working
who did you share your stimulus package with, Juanita?
another loutish sportsman has disgraced himself in public
Juanita, let the sports reporter read that stuff in future
debate continues about the best way to tackle climate change
if we had an ETS, Juanita, would you trade emissions
    with me?
she is telling me that tomorrow it will be warm and moist
and Jesus Christ, Juanita has two buttons undone on
    her blouse

there will be a news update in an hour
but not from Juanita Cox
and without Juanita Cox
no news is good news.

Mass in the West of Ireland

The men in their shiny arsed suits
gather close to the door
inhale the incense, the mothball aroma
of their neighbour's Sunday best
endure the droning of the priest
who denounces the idleness of men
the sinfulness of women
they feel ferocious thirsts building
their minds wander to the pub
where the publican is pulling pints of porter
letting them stand, almost full, on the bar
foaming, settling, forming voluptuous heads
waiting for the appreciative lips, mouths, tongues
of the restless church bound men
one breaks ranks, slinks out the door
the others look sheepishly at each other and sidle, dribble
across the road to slake their thirsts
knowing that they have, barely, done their duty for the week
they can, with an almost clear conscience,
drown their sins in the landlord's best beer.

Synergy

On Cross Road, Adelaide, is a business
whose sign proclaims to the passing traffic:
>   *Dentures and Colon Irrigation*
for some reason it makes me smile and grimace at the
>   same time
I imagine the waiting room
some gritting their false teeth
some squeezing their buttocks together
is it the same technicians, I wonder, who service both sets
>   of clients?
do they alternate "tooth days" with "arse days"?
and if they do both jobs on the same day,
do they do the teeth before the arses
or vice versa?
I'D WANT TO KNOW!
what is the synergy between the two lines of business?
do they get referrals from satisfied denture clients
who know somebody who needs a good clean out of the
>   back passage?
Ooh Vera, I'm so happy with me new gnashers from those nice
>   *people on Cross Road*
p'raps they'd be able to fix up your constipation
and most importantly, do they ever mix up the clients'
>   appointments?
one minute you think you're about to get your new
>   teeth fitted
next thing you're face down with a big rubber hose between
>   your legs
and a jet of hot water squirting up you
you come out feeling down in the mouth but thoroughly
>   flushed.

Incident at Brownhill Creek

On the hobby farm
the man looks fondly on his flock
the dog looks up at the man
the dog looks down on the flock
the man crouches next to one of the sheep
runs his hands through its fleece
the sheep likes this
the dog thinks this is not quite right, growls disapproval
the man playfully pushes the sheep from side to side
the sheep likes this
rolls over, much like a dog
the man is amused
the dog thinks this inappropriate, barks displeasure
the man pats the sheep's stomach
the sheep likes this
throws its head back, wriggles with joy
the man is delighted
the dog thinks this is outrageous, runs around yelping
    his fury
the man comes to his senses
looks at the dog sheepishly
the dog looks at the man sternly, nips the ankle of the sheep
steers it back to the flock, returns to sit by the man's heel
looks up at the man
order is restored.

The Wind off the Thames

Winter Saturday afternoon 1960s London
the tube to Hammersmith station
electric magnetic acrid ozone
escalate from underground below the flyover
two miles walking redbrick backstreets
two shillings entry to

struggling Fulham football club
the riverside stand terraced with men
in solitary union, a fug of damp overcoats
sweat, cigarette smoke, Brylcreemed heads
sweet scalding tea, steak and kidney pies
fortify against the wind cutting off the water

another loss to a better team, in my despond
spill from a desolate stadium to trudge
the lonely drag back home
envy others starting out early evening
more human, rewarding, alliances, affinities
than devotion to a football team

40 years later on the far side of the world
unable to sleep I rise to watch
an internet stream a pixellated view
an all seater covered stadium
smoking forbidden, pomaded hair passé
but the same disappointment

I return to a bed as cold
as the chill wind off the Thames.

Cooking with My 14 Year Old

My son and I have made a deal
he stays in our house rent free
so long as he helps with the evening meal

side by side we talk, dice, slice
potatoes, sport, TV
carrots, music, advice

I could delegate the whole thing
feet up, cold beer
and be waited on like a king

or let him play a video game
cook on my own
he wouldn't complain

but the food tastes better
is more nourishing
when we work together

there's more fun
more warmth in the kitchen
when I cook with my son.

On Goolwa Beach

the waves are
dogged
bounding
puppies bouncing
excitedly around your feet
Greyhounds sprinting in to nip your
ankles   Labradors wet nosed gambolling
slobbering   Rottweilers snarling slavering
knocking you off balance   in packs   hard
on the heels of the leader   sex crazed
sniffing the one in front   mounting it
mad   things   collapsing   foaming retreating
whimpering spent on the sand   cowering like whipped curs.

Wilson Tuckey, I Love You Man

Wilson Tuckey, I love you man
the way you look over your glasses
as you kick those journos' arses
I love your hairy nostrils and your square double chin
but most of all I love the way you know everythin'
not a skerrick of doubt, any subject, any time
you can hold forth, you're ready to chime

Wilson Tuckey, I love you man
you don't need no research, no need to hold back
here is your wisdom, you're on the attack
here is the gospel according to Tuckey
you front them with macho, you front them so plucky
you tell them the answers straight from the heart
they look like stunned mullets as you take them apart

Wilson Tuckey, I love you man
you run rings round those greenies, those tree hugging scum
with their talk about warming, their climate change glum
I trust you Wilson, you know better than them
you can leave them all gobstruck with a home spun gem

Wilson Tuckey, I love you man
you can spot a terrorist at a hundred paces
the ones with the beards and the slightly dark faces
we don't want them here taking our jobs and houses
with their Qurans and burqas and baggy white trousers

Wilson Tuckey, I love you man
you show us what it means to be Australian
some call you redneck, some say you're not cool

but you are our bedrock, you are no fool
you are the brown substance of this wide, sunburnt land
and that's why, Wilson Tuckey
I really, really, really love you man.

Dementia Ward

– The quotes are the words of residents of a dementia ward

In the garden of the dementia ward
gazing over the fence, she says
I want to go home
but I don't know where
and I don't know how

In the recreation room
tapping rhythms
on the table, he says
every subject of music is in my ears

In the corridor
in a wheelchair
face to the wall, she wails
where's my son, I want my son

In the car park
I sit thinking what life would be like
without my most important memories

then

I drive home to my family
listening to the radio
drumming my fingers
on the steering wheel
all the way.

Thoughtlessness

You begin to think something might be wrong when your son calls you a thoughtless, self-centred bastard. You forgot his football match for the second week running. Hell, you give him good pocket money every week. What's he got to complain about? Thoughtless? Your ex-wife recently told you she decided to leave when you didn't take your eyes off *The Sopranos*, as she told you her father had died. You think back, recalling that more than one girlfriend got upset about you neglecting to open the car door for her *like a real gentleman would*. Others complained about you leaving the toilet seat up, squeezing the toothpaste tube in the middle and leaving a high tide scum line of shaving soap and bristles in the sink. Trivial stuff. You don't get to be a corporate leader and a pillar of society by worrying about trivia. Oh no. But just to be on the safe side, tomorrow you'll get your personal assistant (what IS her name?) to buy a copy of *Thoughtfulness for Dummies*. She can read it in her lunch break and tell you what the key messages are. Tonight though, there's a rerun of *The Sopranos* to catch.

Dem Old Writer's Block Blues

Well I woke up this morning
I had those writer's block blues
said I woke up this morning
had those old writer's block blues
couldn't write a single word
lord, I completely lost my muse

well I woke up this morning
had a deadline to meet
said I woke up this morning
poetry competition deadline to meet
couldn't even fill in the entry form
lord, my writing hand felt so weak

got them writer's block blues
meanest blues I ever had
got them writer's block blues
meanest blues I ever had
no Ted Hughes, Yeats or Wordsworth
ever suffered dem blues so bad

well I woke up this morning
to that poetry group I had to go
said I woke up this morning
to that old poetry group I had to go
had to face dem other fancy poets
with all their shiny new poems on show

well I woke up this morning
'nother rejection in the mail
said I woke up this morning
'nother rejection in dat mail
bin 13 years submitting poems
still don't have one that didn't fail

well I went to the poetry slam
went and told them my best poem
well I went to the poetry slam
went and told them my best poem
those performance poets they so young and cool
felt like I should be in an old folks' home

got them writer's block blues
meanest blues I ever had
got them writer's block blues
meanest blues I ever had
no Larkin, Blake or Seamus Heaney
ever suffered dem writer's block blues so bad
said no Ted Hughes, Yeats or Wordsworth
ever suffered dem writer's block blues so bad

mmm . . . mmm . . . mmmmm . . .

The Template

Another soldier dead. Pull out the template and we'll knock off the story in a flash. First the headline words. "Digger" and "fallen" are mandatory. "Brave" and "salute" are excellent accompaniments. Slap 'em on the front page. Big and bold. Now, keep the report's body simple. No need to mention that he was scared of dying. He was a brave soldier, willing to face danger in the service of his country. Competent? Who knows? So just say he was dedicated and professional and served with distinction. If he was SAS or a paratrooper then he's always, always "elite". He might have been a pain in the arse. But the template says he loved his mates and was loved in return. He liked a beer and a laugh. Then fill in the bit about the effect his death will have on the war. Like this: "It increases our determination to see the job through to the end, to fight terrorism abroad so we don't have to fight it on our doorstep". A discreet picture of his wife or girlfriend is very touching. The template has a nice big space for that. Get a shot or two of the politicians in the pews and comforting the next of kin outside the church. After all they've sacrificed their precious time to attend the service, and they like to see that we've stuck to the template.

Glowing in the Dark

Simon J. Hanson

Simon Hanson lives in a small country town in the
South East of South Australia, with his lovely wife and
children and several animals that his kids insist are also
family members.

He has spent a good portion of his life studying philosophy
at Flinders University, relishing the luxury of those years
contemplating life, the universe and pretty well anything.

He attempted to hang onto this lifestyle for as long
as possible, but eventually this gave way to a career in
education. Poetry has now become his preferred means for
getting about the universe and slowing down enough to
admire some of the sights and wonders along the way.

Thank You

Thanks to John Miles for his thoughtful consideration and generous comments.

Thanks to Anne Hanson, my sister, for our much valued exchanges of ideas and poetry and for introducing me to The Gawler Poets, giving me the opportunity to share in their enthusiasm for writing. *Sparklers* is for her.

Thanks to Maggie Emmett: she has been a wonderful source of encouragement since I first came in contact with Friendly Street Poets. Her insightful suggestions have made this a better collection.

Thanks to Thom Sullivan for his much appreciated assistance, insight and expertise in editing this collection. I have been astounded by his commitment to this process.

And thanks to my wife Kylin, my very best friend – always an inspiration to me.

Dedication
For Mum and For Dad
Hoping I can give you both a little bit back . . .

Contents

Ripples

A stillness
dark and deep
a subterranean pool
became a sinkhole
when the roof fell in
centuries ago

and there below
reversing the scene above
a lit circle of blue sky
a drifting cloud
and myself leaning over
looking up

a stone I threw
a disturbance
into the depths of calm
saw it fall
and its image rise

colliding head on
rippling the sky
circles across the surface
ripples through my mind . . .

Sparklers

I still recall your face
aglow with firelight
and wonder
like little magicians
waving our wands of fire
making circles, spirals
figures of eight
in sparkling lines of silver

tiny transient stars
flew along the curves
we drew in the sky
and there too
we signed our names
into the darkness

there was magic flaring
on those pieces of wire
burnt into memory
sparkling in the night
all those years ago.

Elevator

The metal doors slid open
and a woman in a uniform
speaking in a strange voice
appeared
she pressed buttons
took us up and down
up and down to other worlds
each with a different view
and different smells
and different people standing there
she kept saying odd things
about manchester, haberdashery
electrical goods and ladies underwear
and as the doors shut
and the numbers on a dial lit up
away we went
with a strange feeling in our tummies
all rather weird
when you are just four.

Spinning Top

It's been packed away for years
this old tin spinning top
with a plunger in the centre
to make it turn
and a small friction wheel inside
that threw out trails of sparks
like a Catherine-wheel as it spun

painted silver with red and yellow streaks
that merged as it turned
to become an orange spiral
turning now in my memory
and all sorts of things come flashing back

so I give it a whirl
like the flying saucer
I imagined as a boy
around and around it spins
the painted streaks
become an orange spiral
and the sparks, a galaxy twirling

into a time warp
out there in deep space
spinning around and around
then with a fatal wobble and veer
the sparks subside
orange becomes yellow and red
and the spiral is gone.

Distant Moon

A fantasy comes to mind
images of a place, faraway
that I wonder
might somewhere be real

among the billions
blazing in silver, a single star
a nameless planet
and its nameless moon
windswept
deathly cold

its skyline at night
black on black
dotted by distant lights
over vast plains of stone
where the winds' wild howling
has never been heard

and with the rising of its sun
a great shadow recedes
leaving those plains
glittering
with a crystalline frost
that has never been seen.

Sequins

Before the glow of flames
and the light of a lamp
upon her work
she sits sewing sequins
onto her daughter's dancing
costume

charmed by symmetries
shimmering before her eyes
her mind in reveries
adrift in memories
of a dress she once wore
decorated with Indian beads

the sequins of turquoise and silver
flashing peacock colours
with every movement
and turn of her head
she finds herself drawn
to the edge of trance

and dreams of a dancer
in diamonds and pearls
whirling in rainbows
a pirouette of fire
ablaze
in a glittering arabesque.

Hallucination

Collapsing onto my bed
giving myself up
to the sleep of the dead
through each degree
in a radial arc
I fall
through each angle
a second hand ticking
I drop
as if lit by a strobe light
flashing
silhouettes pulsing
almost in x-ray

onto the mattress
I plummet
then through it
through the floor
and into a dream
the world has become

adrift in a space infinitely vast
drifting toward a distant light
shining citrine
a loud click
time is suddenly frozen

and there beside me
a door . . .

Grandma's Uranium Glass

I love to recall your cottage by the sea
and the coolness of your kitchen
its curtains drawn against the summer heat

your fondness for green glass
that bowl and matching vases
the jug from which you poured cordial
made cold with crushed ice

a most treasured piece
the mermaid among the waves
there on your round table
the shadow of your lace curtains
casting a delicate net over her
as the afternoon hours drifted by

it's all in my house now
displayed in a cabinet
glowing under a black light
this light of deepest violet

rays fluoresce the glass
radiant in cool electric green
setting my lounge aglow
with a light from another world
another time.

The Other Side

by an orchestration
of orbits and rotations
we only ever see
one side of the moon

around the other side
away from our gaze
a place
that never looks back at us

up into that black sky
devoid of the earth
a crystalline view
bejewelled in a billion stars.

Abyssal Zone

Down
and further down
plunged in darkness
under miles and miles of sea
live strange and fabulous things
down gaping trenches
along ledges
and around rocky spires

there are things down there
creeping and crawling in mud
or swimming
in black water just above
things beautiful and grotesque
some with long needle teeth
and bulbous eyes
fish wearing lures and lanterns
flickering, flashing
jellies pulsing with colour
sea stars, worms, mussels, crabs
tiny things and large
living in the depths
way, way down
in the abyssal zone.

The Rabbits

Rabbits keep getting in
through my back fence
nibbling cabbages
uprooting plants

they come
under cover of darkness
when I'm inside the house
sound asleep

sometimes I see them
hopping around in my dreams
up to their mischief
doing rabbity things

so I repair the perimeter
and chase them away
but the next night
there they are again

through a weakness in my fence
or a fresh tunnel underneath
playing havoc in my garden
again and again.

Phantoms in DNA

What's all the fuss, old boy?
such a ferocious growl
wolfing down your meal
in such a ravenous rush
it's just a visitor at the gate
do you fear they're coming
to snatch your food away
creeping
down those long corridors
of instinct
and ancient memory
where imaginary lions
and hyenas
lay hiding in the grass
stalking you still
after thousands of years
planning to thieve your kill
(though you are hardly a hunter now
are you, old fella?)
do you expect them
as you turn snapping
glaring behind
at those ghosts
from another time?

Time beneath Our Feet

The autumn leaves swirl
over the compost beneath
last season's life, fallen
upon a soil of many years below

further down
the clay of centuries past
littered with the relics of life
long decayed
under every step, over stone
of a hundred thousand years

down through the layers
of years in their millions
imprints marking the tread
of ancient animals roaming
fossils of fin, feather
shell and bone

further down into the eons
of ages crystallised in fire
geometries lay long hidden
deep within the Earth

upon eras and eons we walk
with time beneath our feet.

The Long Winter Night

Gathering the kindling
a practice as old as humanity
dry twigs and sticks to start our fire
in a fireplace of steel and glass

and branches too I forage and break
carry them back to where we'll sit
as it has been done for ages past
this time in my home dwelling

the logs I chop and stack
will keep us safe and warm
will keep the wolf from howling
here at my suburban door.

Fire Circle

In the flicker of fire
ancient things eddy and rise
ancestral histories
burn deep inside
flaring violet and blue
where voices
talk of the day's hunt
laid upon the coals
with murmurs of ceremony
and stories told under stars

held by visions, almost seen
a circle of ecstasy turns
hand in hand
under the moon
chanting can be heard
and the eyes of the forest
gaze on those lit
by a flickering orange glow
and sees their shadows
dancing on the great stones.

Geometrical Spaces

On the internet last night
an intrusion of the numinous
geometrical fascinations
in two and three dimensions
with a touch of keys
polygons and polyhedrons
trickled down through cyberspace
and into my screen

selected from a dropdown menu
the forms came in colours
stunning electric hues
triangles, pentagons, pyramids
and prisms
jewels afloat in the void of space
descending into my darkened room

then an apparition
the Sphere
formed in dots along gridlines
on the ghost of a globe spinning
clockwise and then counter
its speed adjusted
by a slide-bar setting

an alchemist dabbling in the night
phosphoresce glowing in a flask of light
the Sphere radiant in electric blue
slowly turning to those eerie sounds
Dark Side of the Moon.

Little Black Fish

facing upstream
each and every one
content it seems
to rest on
the pebbles beneath
while the stream
slides over them
in silver ribbons of light.

Cuttlefish

Behind plate glass
lying limp on stainless steel
its eyes fixed in an empty stare
snared the night before
life and colour ebbed away.

What a difference life makes . . .
this very morning
I saw three of your cousins
ethereal ambassadors from another world
they jetted in, suddenly poised
fluttering in waves of grace
flashing iridescent.

Liquid lightning, watery spirits
at one with the sea, a melody of motion
with a sudden flush of magic
they donned their camouflage
in unison they went
swift as arrow shot – disappeared
into the distant darkening green.

I paid for the cuttlefish on the tray
covered it in bread crumbs
lightly fried in virgin olive oil.
That night I dreamt of deep sea cuttlefish
ten thousand of them on the move
lighting up the inky depths
in a ghostly luminous glow.

Limestone

Our house is built from sea shells
coral and the bones of fish
pressed in these blocks of stone
once the bed of an ancient sea
their remains laid to rest

in this house last night I dreamt
of Silurian seas alive
turquoise waters and colourful fish
plankton and coral reefs
life teeming in its trillions

one by one they fell
upon the sea floor
in these stones brimming of the past
so many stories cradled within
stories in want of telling

and with the fall of night
on the shores of sleep
adrift among these stories
I wonder if these stones
might whisper to me again tonight.

Starfish

Through the clouds
flying swift
in silvered blacks and greys
the moon shone through
there in the shallows
five pointed, violet coloured
a starfish did too
bent upon a reefy ledge
partly hidden in shadows
partly hidden in the leafy swirls
of pallid greens and browns
and as the clouds flew
across the sky
so the colours
on that half dark night
occasionally withdrew
but not long after
through clearings in the sky
soft luminous fingers
delved again
among the shadows
and leafy swirls
revealing
that pale glimmer of violet.

Fleeting Moments

Sky and sea
merged as one
the horizon hidden
in a wash of grey
blended with a splash of orange
and in shimmers of purple and pink
an old time schooner lay
dissolving in the sultry heat
in a mingling of air, light and water
merging
with memories.

Sea Lights

Slow and steady she went
cleaving loose furls of water
to either side, starboard and port
and in that foamy tumble and curl
the glowing spirals and swirls
of phosphorescent plankton
little lights busy scribbling
luminous lines in the dark

wondering
what was to be seen astern
there I went
and in that foamy wash
spread soft and broad
into the darkening distance
thousands of tiny lights
in an effervescent flicker
in the wake and trail behind.

Fish Pond

Ledges of stone
cast their cool shadows
into the watery space below
Arum lilies, lilacs and violets
spilling over the edges
drink at their own reflections
those flowers made of light

in a flash of gold
in the flick of a fish's tail
these flowers are set in motion
in a trembling of greens
purples and whites
till they are held once more
in the stillness of the pond.

Calm

out on the Pacific

one tropical night
southwest of Suva

where the horizon
circled the sea

and a domed sky
strewn with stars

stars that shone again
in the sea's dark mirror

we drifted, becalmed
on a rhythmic swell

gently rising and falling
with the ocean

as if the great sphere
were breathing.

Above and Below

Curious I thought
curious I felt
drifting off to sleep
a crocodile's eye view
it seemed
partially submerged
glimpsing
in a single moment
the world above
and the world below
the waterline.

Within

You stand whole and complete
but with a microscope
a single cell I could observe
one of your trillions

if I could shrink down
and around a spiral of DNA
I could slide
into the chemistry
of your body
stardust they say

a shimmering lattice
of electrical forces
a whirl of particles
pulsing billions of times
every second

and there clothed
in the fabric of the universe
with histories reaching back
to the beginnings of time
from mystery to mystery
into the fathomless deep

there you stand
sacred
One with all things.

Friendly Street New Poets Series

Friendly Street New Poets 9 (2003)
Peeling Onions • Jill Gloyne
Crescent Moon Caught Me • Judith Ahmed
Scoffing Gnocchi • Linda Uphill

Friendly Street New Poets 10 (2004)
Stealing • Libby Angel
Deaf Elegies (from Virginia Woolf's Record Store) • Robert J. Bloomfield
Sparrow in an Airport • rob walker

Friendly Street New Poets 11 (2005)
low background noise • Cameron Fuller
words free • Simone G. Matthews
jars of artefacts • Rachel Manning

Friendly Street New Poets 12 (2006)
The Night is a Dying Dog • Steve Brock
Travelling • Margaret Fensom
Nectar and Light • Murray Alfredson

Friendly Street New Poets 13 (2007)
Black Magic • Courtney Black
Circus Earth • Janine Baker
Hieroglyphs • Roger Higgins

Friendly Street New Poets 14 (2008)
Snatching Time • M.L. Emmett
The Boy Full of Broken Promise • Rob Hardy
Airborne • Thom Sullivan

Friendly Street New Poets 15 (2009)
A Lesson in Being Mortal • Louise McKenna
A Pause in the Conversation • Lynette Arden
Natural Intervention • Sher'ee Furtak-Ellis

website: friendlystreetpoets.org.au
email: poetry@friendlystreetpoets.org.au
postal: PO Box 3697 Norwood SA 5067